ISBN 978 0-692-76310-0

Published by Recuerdos Press
PO Box 387
Warner Springs, CA 92086
Rockhilllearning.com
rbrujo@sbcglobal.net

Cover: The Fredrick Grand wine vault in Arkansas Canyon.

This book is dedicated to all of the wine grape growers and wine makers of San Diego County – past, present, and future. You have taken a path that is often difficult across a landscape that does not always reward you with the fruits of your labor. And yet when the wine on the lees is well refined we all enjoy your efforts with great pleasure.

Of Wine on the Lees Well Refined: A History of the Wineries and Wines of San Diego County

Richard L Carrico

Preface

All books have their most basic origins in the fertile mind of some author, editor, or publisher. This book came about as the result of years of research on topics other than wine and wineries in San Diego. It seemed that whatever the topic--be it local Indian people, famous pioneers, economic development, or local landmarks, the tendrils of vines and wine crept into the picture.

And yet basic research into wine history texts, reviews of historic maps of California's wine regions, and discussions with knowledgeable wine folks produced little information. Sure, some scholars and local Chamber of Commerce types gave a passing nod to the origins of California's wine industry at Mission San Diego de Alcalá. Others noted that somewhere in San Diego County vineyards popped up in the late 1800s and the influx of Italians to the area led to substantial home wine-making. But the story is far more complex than that, with a cast of characters, vignettes, and histories that deserve to be told.

Pull up a glass of your favorite wine, a local wine would be a great and satisfying choice, and take a walk through the centuries old story of San Diego wine and wineries.

Introduction

The lush valleys of Napa and Sonoma are probably the first verdant places that spring to mind of California wine lovers. A combination of effective marketing, excellent wines, and user friendly tourism, have, for decades, propelled Napa and Sonoma firmly into the forefront of our thoughts about wine and wine making. In the past two or three decades, the wine regions of Santa Barbara, the Sierra Nevada Foothills, and Paso Robles have also gained prominence.

But this hasn't always been so. Southern California's wine history and lore began nearly 100 years before the regions north of San Francisco gained grape fame. San Diego County, with its Spanish, French, Italian, and German immigrants, played a significant role in the history of wine and wine making in California. Although little noted today, Valley Center, Ramona, Alpine, Escondido, Vista, and Otay were once the wine capitals of San Diego County and significant wine sources in California. From the expansive vineyards that spread across San Diego County thousands of gallons of wine found their way far and wide. Several miles to the north Cucamonga wine was also well-regarded and considered by many in the 1880-1910 period to produce the finest wines in southern California.

It is no exaggeration to say that southern California and San Diego County's wine roots extend deep into the early Spanish period more than 230 years ago. Until missions to the north of San Diego developed their vineyards in 1774, wine for the early California colonies came from Baja California, mainland Mexico and even Spain. With a history that stretches back well beyond that of Alta California, Baja California has an even longer heritage of wine making that continues to this day.

One Hundred Year Old Head Trained Vines at Rancho La Puerta in Tecate, Baja California

Writers of romanticized California history and San Diego Chamber of Commerce folks often erroneously attribute Father Junipero Serra with planting the first grape vines in San Diego in 1769. While Father Serra may have been administratively involved in wine production several years later, he certainly did not plant vines or even oversee their planting in early San Diego. Mission San Diego de Alcalá was not located at its current site in Mission Valley until 1774, having been founded within the walls of a Spanish fort on what is now Presidio Hill several miles to the west in 1769.

There are no historical records indicating the establishment of vineyards at the Presidio and it is unlikely that the presidial soldiers were tasked to maintain vineyards. After the mission moved to Mission Valley in 1774 Tipai Indians subsequently sacked the mission and it was rebuilt the following year — certainly not an atmosphere conducive to planting acres of vineyards.

So exactly when the Spanish missionaries of Alta California first made wine from locally grown grapes remains uncertain. Most serious scholars would say local wine filled colonist's cups as early as 1781 and certainly by 1782.[1] By 1801 six California Franciscan missions raised so-called "Mission" grapes and pressed wine for local use and for export to those missions and pueblos without established vineyards. For a brief period in the early 1800s Alta California's first mission, Mission San Diego de Alcalá, gained modest fame for its wine. Mission San Diego probably did not, however, produce any wine until after 1781, having received its first vines in May 1778.[2]

From approximately 1781 to 1830 San Diego proceeded to produce large amounts of wine with the heyday probably being around 1820. In 1819, amidst the Mexican War of Independence, Pablo Vicente de Sola, the Spanish governor of California, requested that the San Diego mission send a dozen bottles of wine to King Phillip II of Spain. This shipment served as a form of tribute but also to show the King how successful the colonies were at wine making. Perhaps as an afterthought, Governor Sola, ever the astute politician, also suggested that a barrel of wine should be sent to the viceroy of Mexico, where it was reportedly well-received.

Mission San Diego's spot in the wine limelight, however, quickly faded. San Diego in general slipped into a post-revolution malaise and by 1835 both the Presidio and the Mission were abandoned. Little mention is made of wine or wine making in the sleepy pueblo of San Diego centered on today's Old Town. By contrast, with its extensive vineyards flourishing by

1820, Mission San Gabriel in the Los Angeles basin, soon eclipsed Mission San Diego and ultimately became the primary wine producer for the missions of southern California.

Alta California's First Mission: San Diego de Alcalá

Mission San Gabriel's wine and, more importantly, its more potent rustic brandy, always a staple of pioneer California drinkers, had a large, thirsty clientele. Before the Americanization of California beginning in the 1840s, San Gabriel's vintages were the alcoholic beverages of choice for many Spaniards and Mexicans.

Diaries and travelogues of the period speak well, if not glowingly, of mission wine and brandy.

Yet, even the best California mission wines paled when compared to the vintages of France, Italy, Spain, and Germany. Quality and taste were also trumped by cost and accessibility. Trade restrictions favored wines made in Spain at the expense of California wines. Simply put, the humble Mission grape, although a true *vinifera* with Old World roots (by way of distant Peru), yielded plenty of juice, was easy to grow, but sadly it produced only drinkable, quick to spoil, average tasting wines.

Recent DNA studies have proven that the California Mission grape and its cousins in South America, Pais and Criolla, are genetically the same as Listán Prieto from the Spanish mainland. In that sense the Mission grapes at our California missions literally possessed roots in Spain. Today the Mission grape can be found only on the Spanish Canary Islands west of Morocco and of course in small pockets of the New World, mainly southern California.[3]

Following secularization of the California missions in 1835 and total abandonment a decade later, southern California began a long tradition of non-mission wine and non-Hispanic winemakers. The 5,680 to 8,000 vines reported at Mission San Diego during its heyday were neglected. When Richard Henry Dana author, of *Two Years Before the Mast*, visited Mission San Diego in 1835 in the midst of secularization, he dined with the head priest and enjoyed a decanter of wine. Although Dana did not describe the wine specifically, he called the meal "a regal banquet."[4]

Mission San Gabriel Mass Producer of Early Southern California Spanish Wines and Brandy

Four years later a British officer, perhaps accustomed to the fine clarets from France, was more critical. Captain Edward Belcher of the Royal British Navy came to San Diego and noted that only minimal wine was being made at the mission and what wine there was he deemed seriously inferior.[5] By 1841 the mission itself was crumbling and the vineyards were barely alive and untended. When Santiago Arguello purchased the old mission land grant in 1846 the vineyard was not even listed as a part of the official inventory.

Following the Mexican War in 1846-1848, California became part of the United States and the mission lands were officially surveyed in 1854. No vineyards appear on the official maps either because they had been ripped out or died off--or both. Either way the five decades long practice of wine making at Mission San Diego passed into local lore and history.

Prior to American annexation of California as a territory in 1848, most of the Mexican rancheros on their extensive haciendas made some amount of wine or aguardiente (a distilled spirit also from Mission grapes). After the ill-fated Battle of San Pasqual in December 1846, General Stephen Watts Kearny's wounded and dispirited men trudged past by what is now the Orfilia Winery and vineyards in western San Pasqual Valley.

Further to the southwest they stopped on their way to San Diego at the ranch house of a prosperous Mexican ranchero, Francisco María Alvarado. Alvarado owned the sprawling Los Peñasquitos Rancho. In an early testament to the healthful benefits of California wine, Dr. John S. Griffin, Kearny's assistant surgeon, noted wryly that while resting at the rancho the men procured "a barrel of wine (for the sick and wounded)."[6]

Alvarado Adobe Where Kearny's Men Enjoyed the Healing Properties of Wine

Perhaps wine also played a role in General Kearny's defeat at the hands of Colonel Andres Pico's Californios. Some contemporary observers suggested that several of Kearny's officers suffered hangovers going into the Battle of San Pasqual. They were accused of over indulging in wine or aguardiente at the Santa

María Rancho at present-day Ramona just prior to the disastrous battle.

From its Spanish origins, the wine industry in San Diego slowly branched out. Its growth, and ultimate success, owes a great deal to immigrants from non-Hispanic cultures and countries. As with much of California agriculture, and culture in general, the men and women of Italy, France, and Germany inoculated the southern California wine scene with their practices, tastes, and centuries old wine traditions.

With the takeover of California by the Americans in 1848, wine making received a huge boost. The influx of Americans, English, and Europeans as a result of the California Gold Rush and the opening up of California brought immigrants with a thirst for wine. As early as 1856 an overly optimistic civic booster proclaimed that the "manufacturing of wines and brandies will eventually become the staple of San Diego County." This proved to be marvelous marketing, but poor prophecy.

One early booster, Agoston Haraszthy, often erroneously credited with being the father of California wine making, came to San Diego in 1849 by way of Wisconsin. This flamboyant Hungarian immigrant, who fancied himself a self-appointed Count and sometimes

also a Colonel, owned 160 acres in San Diego's North
County.

The "Count" may have planted a few vines and made
wine from local Mission grapes but there is no evidence
that he substantially influenced San Diego's agricultural
history. The "Count's" local claim to fame is that he
served as a sheriff, politician, and constructed the first
American period jail in Old Town--a jail notorious for
the ease of escaping by simply breaking through its
porous concrete walls.

In 1852, only two years after California statehood,
Haraszthy was elected to the new state legislature and
relocated his family north from San Diego in search of
wealth and fame. After resettling in the Sonoma area in
1856, Haraszthy established the still flourishing Buena
Vista winery, planted hundreds of acres in vines, and
with his many trips to Europe, became a strong
advocate for the introduction of European grape
varieties. Haraszthy correctly realized that if California
was to challenge Europe in wine making, it would not
be with Mission or native American grapes.

Family myth and the local press of the time promoted
Haraszthy as the man who brought Zinfandel to
California and who first introduced French varietals.
There is no evidence for this, however, he did raise

awareness about the possibilities of making fine wine based on European root stocks and cuttings. Ever the restless type, the Count moved to Nicaragua where, in 1869 he drown or was eaten by an alligator, depending on the storyteller.

Count Agoston Harszathy
Important Viticulturist, but Not A Founding Father

**Sonoma County's Buena Vista Winery. One of
Harszathy's Enduring Legacies in California**

Far more important than Count Haraszthy, Jean Louis
Vignes, a French immigrant, planted Bordeaux cuttings
in the dusty Mexican pueblo of Los Angeles as early as

1835 and established the Aliso Winery. Producing his first vintage in 1837, when California was still part of Mexico, Monsieur Vignes maintained 104 acres of vineyards where the Santa Fe Depot is located along Los Angeles and Alameda Avenues. Between 1837 and the late 1850s, Vignes developed a wide following for his French style aged wines. Trained in Bordeaux as both a cooper and a vineyardist, Vignes knew that the key to great wine was in growing quality grapes with complexity and then carefully aging the wine in oak barrels.

Vignes' Aliso Winery rapidly became known for aging wine in massive wooden barrels and for making high quality brandy and Angelica. Not common today, Angelica was a wine cordial invented in the mission era. To produce it, Mission grapes were given a retarded fermentation at which point high proof aguardiente was added to fortify the juice.

Typically, but not always, the Angelica would be aged for 8 years, producing a nutty, high alcohol "sweet" and aromatic dessert wine. Supposedly named for Los Angeles, where it originated, and was fostered by Vignes, Angelica remained popular well into the 20th century and is still produced. The Jean Vignes family, including his nephew Sainsevain, who lived for many years in San Diego, also pioneered vineyards in the arid

Cucamonga Valley. These vineyards preceded the better known Secundo Guasti family by several years. At a peak of 40,000 gallons (more than 16,000 cases) in the late 1840s, Vignes' Aliso Winery inspired others to lay out vineyards in the Los Angeles area.

Vignes also patented the Temecula land grant in 1852 with aspirations for planting extensive vineyards there. But when Vignes sold his 26,608 acre parcel in 1853 the new owners were far more interested in cattle grazing than raising grapes. Temecula's opportunity to become California's wine country went dormant for more than a century — but its time would arrive.

Today Vignes' vineyards are a distant memory of southern California's agricultural past. His name, however, lives on as a street name and a major exit off Highway 101 that takes you into the heart of what was once his vineyard in downtown Los Angeles and the birthplace of Angelica.

Early San Diego County: Wines and Wine Making

Between 1850 and 1875 the Los Angeles area gained vinicultural fame as a result of Vignes' brandies and wines. San Diego, however, was slow to develop beyond local home winemakers and persons who maintained small vineyards for both wine and table grapes/raisins. This was due, in part to San Diego's early Mexican and Anglo-American populace who lacked a strong tradition of wine drinking.

Perhaps more importantly, the few vineyards that existed in San Diego and Baja California were propagated with cuttings from the old mission vineyards. These so-called Mission grapes did not make full-bodied wines or one that would last long in a cellar. It would take the introduction of European varietals to jump start the San Diego wine industry.

In 1876 The *San Diego Union* quoted wine grower Mateo Keller whose extensive vineyards were once part of Vignes' in downtown Los Angeles, as saying that there was little demand back east for California wine from Mission grapes. Instead, wines from imported foreign grapes were in increasing demand.[7] With an influx of German, French, and Italian immigrants following the end of the Civil War in 1865 and again in the 1880s the wine scene in San Diego County dramatically changed.

In 1856 San Diego was considered part of the newly formed Los Angeles Vinicultural District along with Santa Barbara, San Luis Obispo, San Bernardino, and of course Los Angeles. The five county District reported 1,213 acres of wine grapes constituting almost 54% of the state total. San Diego however, contributed only six acres. Twelve years later San Diego still reported only 117 acres and approximately 1,500 vines, slightly less than two percent of the District's total.

On the edge of a decade that would see dramatic increases in acreages state-wide, San Diego languished at less than 200 acres for decades. By 1890, however, that number had jumped to 4,627 acres overall for San Diego with more than 465,000 vines but only 132 acres of that number (3%) were reported as wine grapes.

By 1904 acreages continued to mount. San Diego had 5,200 acres in vines constituting almost 19% of the District third behind Los Angeles and San Bernardino. For 1914, the last reported year before prohibition in 1918, San Diego was at almost 13% of the District with 4,340 acres. For most of these years the acreage devoted to wine grapes in contrast to raisin grapes is not listed.

Wine in San Diego County gradually gained some popularity as shown by a large advertisement for the S. W. Craigue & Co. that appeared in the December 1877 *San Diego Union*. Increasingly, San Diego wine makers and wine dealers reached out to the growing wine drinking market. Craigue noted that he carried French wines and that, "California Wines Made a Specialty." Notably, advertisements and broadsides of the time

promoted California wines but make no specific
mention of San Diego wines.

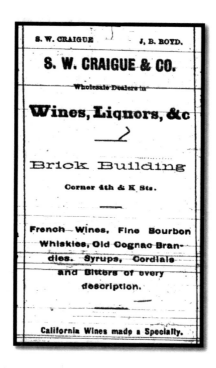

**In the Late 1870s Wine Was Gaining in
Popularity in San Diego**

Which goes to the question of when did the first
commercial winery produce that initial cup of distinctly
San Diego wine?

Valley Center Lays Claim to San Diego's First Commercial Winery

The mists of time cloud for certain who should get the title of starting of San Diego County's first truly commercial winery. It is highly probable that Asher E. (A. E.) Maxcy's vineyards and winery can claim that honor. Maxcy's Vineyard Ranch, near what was then known as Bear Valley and is now Valley Center was the first recorded operation to produce and sell wine. Maxcy immigrated from Massachusetts in 1851 and started farming and ranching in about 1852 with a 360-acre ranch.

Maxcy may have purchased some of the acreage from a Native American 'Ipaay man named Lorenzo who lived there for many years before Maxcy came to the valley.[8] Prior to the arrival of non-Indians, the Vineyard Ranch and Guejito Ranch area was territory shared by the Luiseño to the north and the 'Ipaay to the south. The Luiseño name for the Maxcy Ranch was *shakishmai*, meaning "little nettle" a nod to the stinging nettles that thrived there[9]

Over the next four decades Maxcy expanded his sprawling ranch to more than 4,000 acres. Lacking hard cash, Maxcy made additional land purchases by trading cattle, wagons, and wine to unsuccessful homesteaders or persons with excess acreage. Known as the Vineyard

Ranch, this vineyard and winery was certainly one of the earliest American wine interests in the county although it is uncertain when Mr. Maxcy actually first made and sold commercial wine.

A. E. Maxcy's Abandoned Adobe Winery Circa 1941

Maxey planted Mission and Muscat grapes at an early date but whether they were for table grapes, raisins, wine, or a combination of these uses is uncertain.

If, as some have suggested, a fellow French immigrant Pierre Hagata was Maxcy's first winemaker, the date would have to be after either 1865 when, according to some family histories and secondary documents, Hagata immigrated to America, or after 1873 when Pierre is officially recorded as having immigrated to San Diego from France.

The U. S. federal census for 1900 lists Pierre Hagata as having immigrated to this country in 1873 and lists the number of years in the country as twenty-seven.[10] Assuming that this information was told to the census taker by Pierre himself, 1873 for his arrival date may be accurate and Pierre could have been making wine for Maxcy shortly thereafter. As discussed below, the Maxcy winery ceased operation after Mr. Maxcy's death in 1901 and Hagata worked for others before starting his own operation. By 1911 the Hagata Winery was one of four listed in the San Diego County directory for that year.

The first contemporary mention of Maxcy's winemaking activities appears in an August 28, 1871 newspaper article that noted that Maxcy had just purchased a large wine press and hoped to produce 15,000 gallons of wine that season.[11] Assuming that he had allowed for the vines to reach minimal maturity before harvest, his vineyard may have been planted

Michael Hagata. Second Generation Grape Grower and Wine Maker

about 1868. More conclusively, a newspaper article in September 1871 recorded that Maxcy had 15 acres in wine grapes and 5 acres in fruit trees, and that he had been making about 5,000 gallons of wine for four or five years--so at least since 1867, maybe 1868.[12]

This probably establishes A. E. Maxcy as the first commercial wine maker in San Diego County circa 1867-1868 and assumes that Hagata joined him no later than 1873.

Fifteen acres of grapes would certainly have been sufficient to produce Maxcy's 1871 projection of 15,000 gallons of wine given that an acre can produce approximately 830 gallons of wine. Prior to that a young vineyard would have easily produced the 5,000 gallons Maxcy reportedly made annually between 1868 and 1871. In 1872 Maxcy's wine production fell to 1,600 gallons and the same figure was recorded again in 1879, at which time he said that he was looking to go into commercial sales.[13] This would seem to indicate that although he started a commercial interest as early as 1868 and had made sufficient amounts of wine to market in 1871, he entered into large scale sales in 1879.

In 1881, the *San Diego Union* noted that Maxcy was in San Diego for a visit and stated that the Maxcy vineyard was probably the oldest in the county.[14] That same year Maxcy must have had a surplus of wine grapes given that he advertised that he had 100 tons of wine grapes for sale at a price of a penny a pound or about $20.00 per ton.[15] This price was consistent with the price asked for well-respected grapes from Cucamonga.[16]

Wallace Elliott's *Illustrated History of San Diego and San Bernardino County* completed in 1882, clearly shows acres of vineyard on the Maxcy Ranch that appear to be mature.[17]

Pierre and Alcantara Hagata and Family Circa 1898

By 1883 Maxcy's operation was large enough to warrant investment in better storage and fermentation facilities. Following the 1883 harvest, Maxcy took delivery of ten large wooden wine casks that had arrived on the ship

Orizaba in October.[18] Capacity of the casks is not
provided but they were probably at least 200 gallons,
not the 55 gallon aging barrels that are more common
today. Consistent with Maxcy's wine production, the
ten casks would have held approximately 2,000 gallons
of wine.

Maxcy obviously planted extensive acreage in grape
vines, but it is unlikely that Mr. Maxcy actually planted
1,500 acres of wine grapes as some historians have
suggested.[19] At approximately eight tons per acre
Maxey's 1,500 acres of vines (which would have
hypothetically contained a mind-boggling 1.5 million
vines) would have produced a staggering 600,000
gallons of wine--not likely.

More likely is that the source that stated Maxey had
planted 1,500 acres in vines is seriously in error—either
a decimal point was off and the acreage should be 15
acres or the reference is to the number of vines, which
would be a more realistic 1,500 vines. By comparison
and as discussed below, Emanuel Daneri who was
known to have a very large operation at Otay in the late
1800s and early 1900s produced 20,000 gallons of wine
and the entire Otay Valley put out 30,000 gallons.

It would seem more plausible that Maxcy may have had

between 15 and 150 acres in wine grapes and might have produced between 5,000 and 15,000 gallons of wine--a substantial quantity. Maxcy would have had the labor to produce a prodigious amount of wine.

Maxcy had Indian servants and seasonal Indian workers from the area--primarily 'Ipaay from San Pasqual Valley to the south and Luiseño from the reservations along the nearby San Luis Rey River. During the September 1897 harvest several Luiseños from the Rincon Reservation took part in the picking.[20] The use of Indian labor was common throughout southern California including at the Vignes ranch in Los Angeles.

Maxcy's relationships with his Indian workers and with some of the local Indian women echoed white plantation owners in the American South. According to one historian, Maxcy conducted an extensive illicit trade with the San Pasqual Indians selling them wine and brandy in spite of it being against California law.[21] He could also be a harsh employer and in violation of state law that protected Indians, allegedly using severe whipping as punishment.[22]

Maxcy's checkered sexual relations with Indian women and his treatment of children from those relationships have been documented in a variety of sources. Around 1885 he took a "contract wife," Vicenta Lachusa, a

Luiseño from the nearby La Jolla Reservation. She bore three mixed-blood children whom she took with her when she left Maxcy because of his many infidelities. Upon Maxcy's death in 1901, his mixed-blood children contested his will that left his substantial estate solely to his white daughter.

Consistent with the times, in 1903 the Luiseño children's suit was found by a judge to be without merit because there was no clear documentation of Maxcy's marriage to Lachusa. Therefore they were considered to be unlawful and not legal heirs.[23] By this time Maxcy's legitimate daughter and her husband (a tea totaling temperance advocate) had ripped out the decades old grape vines or allowed them to die off and discarded the winery equipment in a nearby canyon.

In addition to Maxcy's commercial efforts, other early wineries in the county at the time included Juan Forester's at Rancho Santa Margarita, founded circa 1872, Emanuel Daneri in 1878 of Otay Mesa, followed closely by Theophile Verlaque of Ramona in 1880.

Making Wine at Camp Pendleton?

Little is known about the vineyards and winery operated by John (Juan) Forster at his Rancho Santa Margarita. Forster was an Englishman who married into the powerful Pico family that boasted of having generals and governors in their lineage. As a result of favorable political connections, he once controlled Rancho La Nación (now National City) and Rancho San Felipe in the San Felipe Valley in the desert east of Julian. Later, having lost those ranches as a result of loans he took out against them, he and his Mexican wife Isadora took over ownership of the Rancho Santa Margarita from his brother-in-laws Andres and Pio Pico in 1864.

Some poorly documented sources say that the first vineyards on the Rancho Santa Margarita rancho were planted by the Franciscan priests from Mission San Luis Rey after its founding in 1789. Why the good friars would plant vineyards so far from their mission, which already had extensive on-site vineyards, is unclear. What is more certain is that as early as 1872 Forester was successful enough that he shipped two large casks of Santa Margarita wine on the steamer *California* to be sold in San Francisco.[24] In 1879, about five years before the photograph below was taken, John Forster reportedly produced 1,200 gallons of wine from his rancho vineyard and marketed it in both San Francisco and San Diego.[25] Today Forster's Rancho Santa Margarita is incorporated into the Marine Corps Base, Camp Pendleton where his adobe home serves as the Commandant's quarters and a museum.

Rancho Santa Margarita Vineyard in 1883

Otay Valley and the South Bay

In 1878, many miles to the southeast of Rancho Santa
Margarita, Emanuel Daneri developed a 320 acre farm
in Otay Valley below Otay Dam in the South Bay area.
The Otay Valley, with its coastal Mediterranean terrior,
supported a large Italian community and for nearly
forty years produced more wine than anywhere else in
San Diego County. Joining Daneri in running successful

Otay Valley wineries were the Guatellis, Phillipo Poggi and a host of other Italian vintners.

The Daneri Winery in Otay Valley was one of the largest, longest lived, and best known wineries for more than thirty years from 1880 until tragedy struck in the form of a massive flood. Emanuel Daneri, an Italian immigrant, came to America in 1865 from Genoa, Italy and in 1874 opened an unsuccessful restaurant in what was then called New Town — now downtown San Diego. He then tried, with some success, gold mining in Baja California where his tremendous physical strength and stamina were almost legendary. Returning to San Diego with enough money to buy some land Daneri settled into a life of farming, wine making and civic leadership.

In 1878 Daneri planted extensive vineyards and built a large scale winery south of present day Otay Valley Road just east of I-805. The winery was largely built underground with a stamped earth floor, thick cement walls, and massive concrete vats. The cellar measured almost 1800 square feet and replaced an earlier, smaller cellar.

Daneri proudly became a naturalized citizen in 1885.[26] An 1889 newspaper article noted that Daneri received a train carload of 1,000 gallon capacity wine casks from

San Francisco and that he intended to produce 10,000 gallons of wine from the 1889 harvest. The article, perhaps tainted with a little hyperbole, estimated that Otay Valley alone would produce 30,000 gallons of wine that year including 3,000 by Guatelli and 6,000 from Poggi's vineyards. In an 1890 newspaper article Daneri said he actually made about 6,000 gallons of wine from the 1889 harvest and that Zinfandel was one of his main varieties.

As Shown Here, Wine Was Often Sold in Large One Gallon and Two Gallon Clay Jugs

By 1903, Daneri with about 100 acres in wine grapes produced 20,000 gallons of both sweet and dry wine.

Daneri made aged red table wine and distilled special brandies for friends and business acquaintances. Many a San Diego old timer remembered the Daneris for their famous "Tourmaline Wine," named after the local gemstone found near Pala in northern San Diego County, and appropriately described as a beautiful pink.

Sometime before 1904 Daneri purchased the "Our Family" wine store in downtown San Diego from Albert Eicke, a German immigrant, and expanded into retail sales outside of the Otay winery location. Operating at 532 Fifth Street as "E. Daneri and Son, Daneri's Otay Winery and Distillery Depot" they advertised frequently in the *San Diego Union* newspaper.

In a precursor to today's wine tasting rooms, one Daneri advertisement in 1904 offered free samples of wine. As a special treat to his regular customers he also poured generous portions of a 14-year old port. That same year, the *San Diego Union* reported that San Diego was home to five prosperous wineries, unfortunately the names of the companies were not provided. Based on a city directory, the other wineries probably included Brabazon and Scheppelle of Alpine, and Hagata of Vista.

Emmanuel Daneri Regularly Advertised His Wines and
Brandies. This Ad is from 1902

- 37 -

Daneri Wine Cellar Circa 1900 with Demijohns on Floor

Not simply rural farmers and wine makers, Daneri and his wife Rosa lived on the edge of downtown San Diego at 109 15th Street. In 1913 Daneri commissioned local architect Perley Hale to design a steel girded four-story combination winery, hotel, and retail store on his Fifth Avenue lot. The original urban wine shop on the back lot remained, with the new building serving as a façade.

The Otay Winery Advertised Itself as the Oldest in San Diego Having Been Established in 1878

Away from the retail sales in bustling downtown San Diego, Emanuel and his wife entertained hundreds of visitors at their Otay ranch and gave tours of the vineyards and of the refreshingly cool underground winery. One contemporary scribe wrote that after a tour of the Daneri Winery and a near endless tasting of new and aged sweet and dry wines, port, and brandy, one should either stay the evening in the valley or endure a long drunken buggy ride home. No mention was made, or concern expressed, about driving a team of horses while intoxicated through the back roads of southern San Diego County.

Amidst continued prosperity tragedy struck the Daneris and their Otay Valley neighbors in January 1916. As Emanuel Daneri related it, he and his wife Rosa barely had time to run for high ground before a forty foot wall of water swept over the land.

The great flood of January 1916, sometimes known as the Hatfield Flood, intensified by the failure of the Otay Dam, destroyed the Daneri ranch, the thousands of gallons of wine aging in barrels, and the entire winery. Emmanuel said later that as he left the winery for dinner he saw a wall of water coming through the valley. He grabbed his wife Rosa and ran for high ground.

According to his daughter, Aurelia de Bincenzi Daneri, during the flood, "There were great big wine barrels, high as the ceiling, floating down the valley." Several

300 gallon casks were lodged on a gravel bar two miles downstream from the winery.

**A Daneri Wine Tank Discovered Several Miles
Downstream from the Otay Winery**

The newspaper reported that of the 57,000 gallons of wine in storage only 6,000 gallons could be salvaged. The paper also noted cryptically that the military destroyed more than 2,000 gallons of wine to keep order. Human costs were high also; three of the five Daneri employees, Joe and Rose Moste and Carlos Bega, were swept away and killed in the deluge.

**The Styles of Wooden Redwood Wine Casks Used for
Fermentation and Storage between 1870 and the 1940s.
The Cask on the Right which was built in 1909 for
Thomas Vineyards of Cucamonga, Held more than 51,000
Gallons of Wine.**

Heartbroken and devastated, the Daneris retired from
the wine business and never rebuilt the winery. The
legacy of their hospitality and beverage service,
however, thrived for years through their nephews the
Dinis, who ran the well-known and beloved McDinis
restaurants first on Market Street in San Diego and later

in National City. The Daneri name lives on, although misspelled, in Dennery Road and Dennery Canyon in the Otay area. Poggi Canyon is named after the other successful winemaker, Phillipo Poggi of Otay Valley.

A son of Emmanuel, Frank Daneri operated a somewhat notorious roadhouse called the Foothill Lodge near Descanso. In the midst of Prohibition he played an on-going cat-and-mouse game with federal agents.

In May 1926 Frank was arrested for having several gallons of wine and several quarts of whiskey at his establishment in violation of the Volstead Act. At his court hearing Daneri pleaded not guilty proclaiming that the wine was medicinal for treatment of his heart condition. The whiskey, he explained, soothed his aches in the winter when he infused his hot toddies. The judge suggested that perhaps Daneri switch to mountain spring water to comply with the federal law. Daneri paid a fine of $350.00 and resumed his business.

Fenced in by a chain link barrier and nearly covered with weeds and brush, remnants of the Daneri Winery still exist in the Otay Valley in the form of concrete wall fragments and portions of cement vats surrounded by ancient olive trees. The ornate E. Daneri & Sons retail store and hotel, however, still exists intact at 532 Fifth

Avenue in the downtown Gaslamp District, but now sells products other than local wine.

As a historical side note, the Gaslamp District was never illuminated by gas lamps. The neighborhood went directly from oil lamps to electric lights.

Daneri Wine Store and Hotel Building at 532 Fifth Avenue

French Immigrants: Ramona, Julian, and Vista

Daneri probably operated the second oldest successful commercial winery after Maxcy, but a serious contender for the third commercial winery would be Theophile Verlaque in 1879. A French immigrant, Verlaque owned a thriving retail business, ran sheep in the hills of Ramona, ran a store at Warner Springs Resort, and imported wines and liquors. Operating out of his winery first on Sixth Avenue and then at Fifth and Cedar, in downtown San Diego, Verlaque

Warner Springs Ranch Resort Fields

purchased massive wooden wine casks and built a large subterranean wine vault to store his wine.

By 1880, the locally well-known Frenchman was out of sheep herding and devoted much of his time and resources to the wine business. Verlaque, like Vignes in Los Angeles and Maxcy in Valley Center, used Indian labor for the crush, in this case 'Ipaay workers from Mesa Grande and Santa Ysabel. Pre-staging the well-known Lucy Ricardo wine stomping skit, Verlaque reportedly employed French maidens in bathing suits to frolic amongst the *vinifera*. The harvest in San Diego county in 1880 was apparently bountiful with more than 300 tons reported of which Verlaque produced 100 tons.[27]

Verlaque contemplated getting out the wine business in 1881 but apparently had a change of heart.[28] In 1883 Verlaque purchased thousands of Zinfandel cuttings from Leonard J. Rose, a noted San Gabriel Valley wine maker and importer of French and Spanish grape vine grafts. Rose operated the Sunny Slope Estate Winery in what is now Pasadena and was one of the most prominent southern California wine makers from the 1860s to the 1880s. Verlaque's planting of Zinfandel, (also known as Primitivo) in 1883 may have been the first time this grape was grown in San Diego County.

The Zinfandels marked a clear departure from the use of Mission and Muscat grapes for local wines.

Although Theophile Verlaque is credited with establishing the town of Nuevo in 1886, later named Ramona, there is no record of him planting vineyards in that specific area or operating a winery there. He sourced his grapes from El Cajon and Escondido and may have planted his Zinfandels in one of these areas. In 1884, an article in the *San Francisco Merchant* offered positive reviews of what they called a "maiden crop" of Zinfandel from the El Cajon Valley.[29] It is possible that this crop was Verlaque's given that there are no other records of Zinfandel in the county to that point.

By 1888 it appears that Verlaque made good on his desire to yet again change careers and was out of the wine business. He turned his attentions to real estate and retail sales including operating a successful store in Ramona. Always looking for a deal on land and supplies, Verlaque took a partial interest in the hot springs at Warner Springs Ranch. The transaction took place in July 1903, less than two months after the Cupeño Indians had been driven from their ancient homeland.

Verlaque's Ramona residence, with its ramp to roll barrels into the cellar, still stands on the grounds of the

Guy B. Woodward Museum and his Pioneer Store proudly graces Main Street.[30] A pioneer in many ways, Verlaque's name should be associated with promoting the planting of Zinfandel in San Diego County.

The Theophile Verlaque House Ramona, California

A contemporary of Daneri, Verlaque and Forster, French immigrant, Frederick Grand made wine for himself and his East County neighbors in Julian, Banner, and Ramona on a large, but informal scale. As early as 1895 Grand produced wine from vines of an unknown varietal that he planted on the desert side of Volcan Mountain below Julian.

Grand not only made large quantities of wine, he built an impressive stone vault into the hillside to store his wine. Grand bartered his wine for local goods and, as noted in his fascinating diary, a wickered, three gallon, demijohn of wine was usually at his side when he made the arduous trips into San Diego, Julian, or Ramona. Apparently full when he began his trips the demijohn was quite empty when he returned.

Ever the Frenchman, the Frederick Grand wine cave was constructed of hewn stone with large beams hauled down from Volcan Mountain. The gradually curving graceful vaulted ceiling is nearly identical with those in southern France along the Dordogne River.

Today, Frederick Grand's wine cave still exists in Arkansas Canyon within the San Dieguito River Park's eastern property although the 2003 wildfires burned

**Stone Wine Vault of Fred Grand
Built in 1895 in Arkansas Canyon**

most of the wood. His family name is reflected in Ramona's popular Fred Grand rodeo grounds.

West of Julian and Fredrick Grand's vineyards, Ramona, known as Nuevo until 1892, supported six wine grape growers including locally notable men who continued the early efforts of Verlaque the pioneer winemaker.

Three of these men, M. C. Woodson, William Warnock, and Bernard Etcheverry, left their names on streets and as placenames in the community. Doc Woodson, a Confederate veteran, and his vineyards are long gone, but his name is affixed to the rocky mountain that serves as the western gateway to Ramona, to an upscale subdivision, and to a beautiful golf course. Etcheverry's extensive holdings included vineyards just north of Highway 67 near the intersection of Highland Valley Road and Warnock's were east of the town of Ramona on the road to Julian.

Further to the northwest, wine making began in Vista on a large scale in 1884 when two French immigrants, Jules Jacques Delpy and his uncle Bernard Delpy set out several hundred acres of vines. Jules Delpy, sometimes known as Julian, became a naturalized citizen in 1882 and is considered one of the prominent pioneers of agriculture and commerce in Vista.

"Doc" Woodson: An Early Ramona Wine Grape Grower

The Delpy winery was probably the most important commercial winery in northern San Diego County surpassing even Maxcy and Forester. Jules housed his wine press and barrels in an ever expanding winery located at East Vista Way and Foothill, then known to the locals as "Delpy's Corner."

Delpy's Corner in Vista Post-1930

Delpy used redwood vats for initial fermentation, but unlike most wine makers of the period, he imported Spanish oak for aging and storing his wines. He suffered a major setback in November 1902 when his winery burned to the ground.[31] By early 1903, Delpy's new winery emerged from the ashes.

His fellow Frenchman, Pierre (Peter) Hagata, the early winemaker for Maxcy, often worked as the Delpy winemaker and helped his friend Jules Delpy haul grapes from a variety of vineyards including one tucked away in a valley southwest of Rancho Guejito near present-day Lake Wolford, probably Maxcy's Vineyard Ranch.

The hard labor of planting, pruning and harvest at the Delpy vineyards was commonly done by Luiseño Indians from the nearby Pala, Rincon, and La Jolla Indian Reservations. For example, during the harvest on September 18, 1897, Francisco Colol and other Rincon Reservation Indians helped Delpy.[32] These Luiseño laborers also took part in the crush and pressing of the wine. Unlike Maxcy, the Delpy family had a good reputation of treating Indian workers justly and fairly.

As part of the reform measures of the 1890s to control the manufacture and sale of alcohol, state permits were required. For independent wine makers this requirement posed a government intrusion and an added cost, and many simply skirted or ignored the process. In 1897 the long arm of the law reached out. Delpy was tried for selling his wine and brandy without a liquor license. In the following year Delpy was again arrested, this time for selling alcohol to an intoxicated person.

In court Delpy maintained that he was only selling his own self-produced product and was entitled to do so. In an important legal decision for winemakers throughout San Diego County, Judge Torrance found Delpy not guilty and proclaimed that he, and other vineyard owners, were not required to have a liquor license to sell their own product.[33]

Known for his Muscats, which he labeled Buena Vista, or "Beautiful View," Delpy also produced Zinfandel, Maria Port, Muscatel, and Angelica. In what is reputed to have been the first modern distillery in San Diego, Delpy also crafted a highly regarded brandy. Successful for more than 25 years, and at its peak just before Prohibition, the Delpy Winery produced 200,000 gallons a year from his main 40-acre vineyard and from other sources.

In 1915, perhaps foreseeing the gathering clouds of the temperance movement that were ominously rolling across the land, Jules Delpy leased out his Buena Vista winery and vineyards in Vista to A. Valtreda (Valpareda) and V. Campanella, winemakers from northern California. At the time, the *Oceanside Blade* newspaper heralded the Buena Vista winery as one of the oldest and most successful wineries in the state. After the repeal of Prohibition Delpy was reported to be back in the business, and in 1934 had a capacity of 150,000 gallons although it is doubtful that he actually made that much wine.[34]

Italians on the Early San Diego Wine Scene

To the south of Vista and Jules Delpy in Escondido, the Ferrara family established what was arguably San Diego's oldest continuously operating winery until 2013. According to family histories and historical records, the Ferraras took over an extensive vineyard that had been planted as early as 1890 and applied the Ferrara name to the vineyard and the winery.

Born in 1890, George Ferrara immigrated from Italy and he and his wife Sarah operated the Ferrara Winery beginning in 1919. In an interview, Ferrara noted that Prohibition hit him hard, but even so he delivered hundreds of tons of grapes to local families for the legal manufacture of home wines and, of course, for the ubiquitous communion wine for the Catholic Church. Ferrara noted that providing the Church with wine was his civic duty.

The Ferraras grew red and white varieties, and as was common at the time, blended several grape varieties to reach the desired tastes and color. Turning abandoned cattle grazing lands into verdant vineyards, the Ferrara Winery at one time produced a palette pleasing and eye

**George Ferrara: Patriarch of the
Ferrara Winery in Escondido**

popping 29 varieties of wine. The most famous varietal was Muscat followed by a type of Claret, Marsala, and Chardonnay Blanc.

Still in operation until it closed in 2013, third generation Ferraras crafted wine from their 3.4 acre vineyard as well as from other sources. Their Alexandria Muscat was a crowd pleaser as well as their Cabernet Sauvignon, Sauvignon Blanc, Chardonnay, Nebbiolo, and a port style wine. Generations of San Diego wine drinkers supported the Ferrara winery and it is now listed as a Point of Historical Interest.

Another well-known Italian immigrant family can proudly claim title to the oldest vineyard and the oldest San Diego County winery still in operation — the Bernardo Winery. Beginning in 1927 the Rizzos, who emigrated from Italy, began making wine from grapes grown in their extensive vineyards within the old Mexican land grant known as Rancho San Bernardo (now Rancho Bernardo).

The vineyards predated the Rizzo patriarch, Vincenzo, by forty years, having been planted in 1889 by Sicilians. At one time Joseph Mighetto claimed to have founded the winery in 1906. In the early years the winery bore the name Lanza Winery.

FERRARA WINERY

Phone: 745-7632

1120 West 15th Ave.

Escondido, Calif.

Advertisement for Ferrara Winery Circa 1967

Reflecting the palate of their time, Vincenzo and Elizabeth Rizzo's Bernardo Winery, grew Muscat, Mission, Zinfandel, Grenache, Carignane, Mataro (Mouvedre), and Palomino. The use of expensive oak barrels was uncommon in early California wine making. Instead redwood was used by the Rizzo family and by wineries in Los Angeles. The Rizzos struggled during Prohibition. Yet some old timers swore that surreptitious jugs of wine found their way into the trunks of their autos after a picnic at the winery.

WINES BY THE MILLION GALLONS

~~Southern California's~~ Crop ~~Rivals~~
the Yields of France
and Spain.

Five San Diego Firms Make Estimates
of Their Output for the Season —
Heavy Percentage of Brandy
Grapes Insures Big Yield.

**Touting the Advances of Southern California Wine in
1904 and Noting San Diego's Contribution**

Arriving in California in 1861 from Italy Marco Bruschi operated an urban winery in the area of India and Market Streets south of today's Little Italy. He also ran the Mariposa Store at 557 Fifth Avenue near H (now Market) Street downtown and a wine shop at the foot of F Street near San Diego harbor. Facing the same labor shortage as North County wine makers, Bruschi hired Indian laborers during crush season and visitors to the winery recollected barefooted Indians stomping grapes into juice and pulp.

Bruschi's wine was a favorite of the Italian community centered on India Street and was deemed superior to the so-called "Dago Reds" made by others. In addition to operating his own winery, Bruschi also carried wines from other sources including Cucamonga.

As the advertisement below attests, there must have been counterfeit Cucamonga wines being sold and Bruschi sought to ensure the potential buyer know the quality of his wares.

Advertisement July 1871: Wine for a $1.00

Marco Bruschi: Early Merchant and Wine Dealer

Wine and Winemaking Spreads Throughout the County

Several other local wineries and vineyards sprung up in the Escondido and Rancho San Bernardo area in the late 1800s and early 1900s, including George Borra's Borra

Winery (located near Harmony Grove Road), Maghetti, Pio Mighetto, Granchetti, Kuchel, Robert Topi of Coronado (who operated Topi Winery north of Escondido), the Escondido Land and Town Company's holdings, and Frederick Einer. These wineries and vineyards were as different as the emerging wine market they served.

George Borra's Winery Joined the Parade
As Part of the Escondido Grape Day Festival

After graduating from a German trade school, Frederick Einer emigrated from Germany and was naturalized in San Diego County in September 1892.[35]

The Pio Mighetto Winery Float Stressed the Purity of Their Escondido Grapes

Settling in Escondido near Broadway, Einer soon became well known for his sweet, German style wines and fresh vegetables. An adept entrepreneur, Frederick Einer first sold his wine in San Diego by transporting it to the urban center with horse drawn wagons. Later he built a house and small shop on the edge of San Diego Bay; all the better to serve his growing customer base. Following passage of the Wiley Act in 1906, better known as the Pure Food and Drug Act, Einer sold two quarts of his wine without the proper federal permit and was arrested. He paid a small fine and resumed his sales.

One of Einer's best known customers was E. W. Scripps, a gentleman rancher and the owner of a growing newspaper empire that included the *San Diego Sun*. Scripps, who owned a sprawling ranch that is now a subdivision bearing his name, is said to have offered Einer land in exchange for a few gallons of wine. Apparently Scripps was joking or Einer saw no value in the flat, scrubby mesas now covered by the Miramar Air Station and Scripps Ranch; there is no record of land deals between Scripps and Einer. The Einer winery passed into history with the second generation moving onto other ventures.

Wineries of the time made three basic types of wine products: sweet wine, which was actually a euphemism for fortified wine and could run between 16 percent and 24 percent alcohol; dry wines which were unfortified and ran between 11 percent alcohol and 13 percent. Brandy varied from 15 percent to 20 percent.[36] The popularity of "sweet" wines was such that in 1935 they accounted for fully 81 percent of California table wine and as late as 1966 constituted 52 percent of wines sales by dollar amount. Fortunately, our palates have developed and matured since the 1960s. Today, fortified wines (sweet wines) are less than 10 percent of the wines produced in California.

Einer's winery was a relatively small operation for its time and was probably comparable to today's boutique wineries. At his peak in 1880 Bruschi pressed 100 tons of grapes that would have produced about 17,000 gallons of wine.[37] By comparison George C. Kuchel, an Escondido neighbor of Einer, operated a large scale operation producing 52,000 gallons of sweet wine and 7,500 gallons of dry wine in 1903.[38]

Not far from Escondido in the San Marcos/Twin Oaks area, George F. Merriam and Son produced 32,000 gallons of sweet wine and 7,500 gallons of dry wine that same year. Merriam, an heir to the publishing family, noted in 1908 that production of brandy from his grapes was far more profitable than making wine. Both Kuchel and Merriam used Luiseño workers to plant new vines, to prune, and to harvest, particularly in the 1890-1905 era.[39]

Other wineries, owned by investors and absentee land owners, also entered the wine business in the 1880s. In 1885, the Escondido Land Company laid out several hundred acres of Muscat for both table grapes and wine. More in the business of selling land than growing grapes, portions of the Escondido vineyards were sold to outside interests led by the Hagopian & Setrakian Company.

A man with the interesting name of Atpaxat Setrakian was a major force in the California wine and grape industry at the time. Setrakian established the powerful California Growers Winery and Golden State Vintners. With his central base of operations in Tulare, he owned or leased large tracts of land throughout California-- Escondido being one of his smaller holdings. Golden State was one of the largest exporters of wine to foreign markets.

In 1912, a Dr. Cozzoline, about whom little is known, purchased the Escondido Land and Planting Company's winery in Escondido. A chemist with years of experience at the well-regarded Guasti Winery in Cucamonga, Dr. Cozzoline hoped to develop Italian and Spanish grape varieties.

His first venture was grafting Spanish Mataro, a virtually unknown variety in California at the time. In a newspaper interview, an optimistic Cozzoline noted that virtually all his future wine would be sold to the "better" markets on the East Coast. Unfortunately, the fickle wine market and the advent of Prohibition conspired to doom Cozzoline's grand plans.

Raisin Grape Pickers in Escondido Circa 1890

At its peak in the 1880s and early 1900s, Escondido had at least thirteen wineries, including the ones noted above and at least 1,800 acres in vineyards, the majority of which were for table grape production and raisins. Escondido's Annual Grape Day with its parades, dances, and agricultural theme reflected the importance of the noble grape in the region. Communities joining Escondido in having North County wineries and vineyards were San Marcos, Witch Creek, Ramona, Poway, Julian, and Ballena Valley.

**Young Women Posing with Grapes at the
Guasti Vineyards at Cucamonga**

Even the somewhat arid, flat El Cajon Valley and
surrounding hills were home to at least two large scale
wine grape vineyards. Dehesa even boasted its own
winery near the old post office.

In August 1871 Mission grapes of superior quality were
reportedly being harvested from the Ames Ranch in El
Cajon.[40] In 1882 a syndicate of investors headed by men
identified only as Lockwood, Benedict, and Kendall

purchased 100 acres in the Cajon Valley to plant vines and establish a large winery.[41] It is uncertain if their plans ever bore fruit.

In the lush soils of Spring Valley Rufus K. Porter maintained a rustic ranch on the site of an ancient Tipai Indian village. Located just off of Memory Lane and Bancroft Road the ranch house, now known as the Bancroft Ranch House, is a National Register property. Porter was the son of one of the founders of the prestigious *Scientific American Magazine* and maintained an active interest in the science of horticulture and the introduction of new crops to California.

In March 1884 the *San Diego Union* reported that Porter made two barrels (about 110 gallons) of fine Malaga wine.[42] The name Malaga has been associated with both the Cinsault grape and to a lesser extent Semillon. In the case of Rufus Porter's wine it was likely the meaty, red Cinsault.

East of Spring Valley in the back country hills, Alpine became the home of two early successful wineries. Frederick K. Scheppelle (sometimes spelled Chapelle), a Dutch immigrant, ran a winery in Friendship Valley, two miles east of Alpine. His vineyards may have been planted as early as 1880 and produced wine from 1890 to 1911. A well-known local character, Scheppelle was

The Rufus K. Porter/Bancroft Ranch House in Spring Valley, California

unfortunately murdered in 1912 by an allegedly drunken Indian, Indian Charley, during an argument over a jug of wine.

On a much larger scale than his neighbor Scheppelle, George Philip Brabazon, an immigrant from Cork County Ireland, purchased 320 acres in 1885 near what is now the center of Alpine. Brabazon imported

Zinfandel vines (reportedly from Spain but just as likely from L. J. Rose's San Gabriel nursery) to augment an existing smaller vineyard planted earlier by a Fred Overmyer. At an elevation of 1,400 feet, Brabazon appropriately named his winery Monte Vino, or "mountain wine." Typical of the late 1800s, Brabazon hired Indian laborers from the nearby Capitan Grande Reservation to work in his vineyards and to provide bare feet for the time honored grape stomp.

While some of his neighbors may have winced at the image of barefooted Kumeyaays stomping grapes in large wooden troughs, Brabazon's Monte Vino wines, which included Port, Zinfandel, Muscatel, and Riesling, gained fame in Alpine and far beyond. In 1901-1908 Barbazon reportedly exported 30 gallon and 50 gallon barrels of wine to England. Today Brabazon's Monte Vino winery and vineyards have been replaced by apartment houses near the Alpine post office but some of his vines live on in cuttings that have been nurtured at family vineyards.

In addition to some of the grape varieties already noted, other wineries also produced Flame Tokay, Cornichon, and Malvoise (also known as Cinsault) a varietal used in the so-called clarets of the time. All of these wineries shared a limited production and bulk sales in common.

Brabazon's Monte Vino Winery in Alpine

As a group they also prospered between the turn of the century and the era of prohibition beginning in 1920. A growing immigrant population in southern California produced a ready market for their inexpensive wines. Wine commerce in those early days bore little resemblance to today's methods of vinting, storage, aging, and bottling.

Typically, the vineyards were small, the wineries were basic with technologies and tools brought from the Old World, and few wineries bottled their own wine. Instead, wine merchants, the local equivalents of French negotiants, purchased barrels or tanks of wine from the wineries and sold the product to their customers in bulk in small wooden casks or in bottles.

An 1890 Ad for the Wine Rooms That Were Located on H Street between Fifth and Sixth in San Diego

In the time honored European tradition, customers at wineries and wine shops were encouraged to bring their own demijohns, casks, or gallon bottles for filling. Bradley's retail store at Fourth and C in San Diego ran an advertisement depicting a rattan wrapped gallon demijohn with the banner headline "When Empty Let Us Refill." A block south, Klauber & Wangenheim offered wine by "By The Pint or By the Gallon; By The Bottle or By The Case." Up in Vista, the Sandwich Shop quenched thirsts at $.70 a gallon for Claret. In the heart

of downtown Escondido the Golden Peak Wine Barrel
carried a large selection of local wines.

SPECIAL!

CLARET WINE

70c Gallon

Bring Container

VISTA

SANDWICH SHOP

Worly Building, Vista

A popular downtown San Diego wine shop, E. P.
Raether's noted in an 1895 *San Diego Union*
advertisement that "we can bottle your wine order if
you wish," clearly indicating that such bottling was the
exception, not the rule. Even though the firm of S. W.
Craigue in San Diego did not own a vineyard or make
wine, they advertised in June 1873 that they were
prepared to bottle and cork wine with new machinery

and looked forward to serving the needs of the area's wine drinkers.[43] Craigue also carried wine from Cucamonga--genuine Cucamonga wine as the ad below notes.

Smith and Craigue Advertisement 1871for the Ever Popular Cucamonga Wines

It was common in southern California and San Diego during this era to see unlabeled wine bottles or bottles with crudely inked labels on home dinner tables and even at restaurants. Branding, for wine rather than for cattle, was a concept for the distant future.

Local wine prices reflected the diversity in quality and style. Prices in the last decades of the 1800s varied from $.40 to $2.50 per gallon. Brabazon's Alpine Monte Vino Zinfandel went for $1.00 per gallon at the winery and his so called "Dago Red" for $.75 a gallon. Brabazon's son, Montague, remembered a steady stream of customers arriving at the Alpine winery toting gallon bottles and small wooden casks in the years before Prohibition. Einer's Escondido wine sold for $.25 a gallon if purchased directly from him or $.50 from a merchant. Even 100 years ago wine merchant markup doubled the cost of our enjoyment.

Table wine sold towards the low end of the price scale with wines that required aging such as sherries, ports, and Angelica going for a premium. As a frame of reference, a mug of beer went for five cents, an average breakfast on Broadway Street cost twenty cents, and a tailored men's suit set you back $10.00.

An average daily salary for a laborer who worked a ten-hour day was $1.25 with $2.00 a day being towards the top of the labor scale. At that rate an average consumer would have to work two hours to afford a gallon of the lower end of Einer's wine. Adjusted for inflation, the cost for similar quality of a gallon of wine today is still about two hours of wage at minimum wage.

To an immigrant population accustomed to homemade wines or wines made by a local village winemaker, wine was an integral part of life, an accompaniment to food. The Italian, French, German, and Portuguese families who settled in Valley Center, Ramona, Otay, Escondido, Point Loma, San Diego, and throughout San Diego County demanded, and received, wine made in the particular style of their country or region, most often by a fellow ex-countryman.

Besides the grape varieties more common to San Diego County, the northern vintners also produced Sauterne, Hock (a Rhine wine produced from Burger grapes), Claret (often made with Zinfandel and Cinsaut and no relation to true French Clarets) and so-called Burgundy. Joseph Schratn was well known for his German style Rhineland Hock, but the California Burgundy of the time (blends of a wide variety of grapes) bore little semblance to the fine Pinot Noirs and whites of the Burgundy region of France.

By contrast, many of the California Rieslings were highly regarded by the Germanic communities. It was common in this era, and indeed until quite recently, for California wineries to appropriate the name of a famous French or German wine region and label their wines as Burgundies, Champagnes, Gamays, and Rieslings.

Aged wines were not common beverages for the average southern California imbiber. Beneath an advertising headline that read **"Finest Aged California Wines In Stock"**, an advertisement in the 1895 *Son Diego Union* went on to tell the thirsty reader that the "aged" wines were 3, 5, and even 8 years old. Ever on the lookout for the temperance movement and the rising tide of prohibition, advertisements for wine stressed the beneficial qualities of imbibing, one advertisement enthused, "**Drink Wine-Build Up Your Health**."

During this time, the well-established and aggressive Napa and Sonoma wineries began to create some brand identity and quality control by selling their wines to customers in sealed and labeled bottles. Popular brands of the time from the north included Asti, Cresta Blanca, Fleur de Lis, Almaden, and Inglenook. Gustave Niebaum's Inglenook Winery was one of the few to do estate bottling and by the 1890s, as a means of assuring quality, would not sell their wine in bulk.

Cresta Blanca's white Bordeaux and Souvenir wines graced the tables of upper class San Diegans and the finer hotels such as the Hotel Del Coronado and the U.S. Grant. The Cresta Blanca brand had strong ties to San Diego County through its owner, Charles A. Wetmore. Prior to establishing the Cresta Blanca winery in the Livermore district in 1882, Wetmore served as the U. S. Commissioner of Mission Indian Affairs.

In the mid-1870s Wetmore visited the Indians of San Diego and was particularly sympathetic to their plight. Wetmore advocated establishment of Indian reservations and fought for reform within the graft-ridden Bureau of Indian Affairs. Twenty years later, while operating his Cresta Blanca Winery in the 1890s, Charles A. Wetmore invested in the Escondido Land and Town Company. With his knowledge of San Diego County and vineyard management, he may have played a role in the company's planting of their extensive Muscat vineyards--largely for table grapes

South of the border, in 1902, John Hussong, of the now infamous Hussong's Cantina in Ensenada, advertised that he carried fine, healthful wines and the choicest imported champagnes. In efforts to resist Prohibition, another ad told its readers that not only was wine not evil and wicked as the temperance movement declared, it was proscribed in the Bible as the beverage of choice for all classes of men. Now, a hundred years later the health benefits of wine are still the topic of hot debate with most researchers agreeing that wine can play a role in a healthy diet.

Even as the vineyards of San Diego and southern California grew and as California wines began to reflect the attempts of visionaries such as Vignes, LeFranc, Niebaum, Brabazon, and others to make better, higher quality wines, the temperance movement was gaining force.

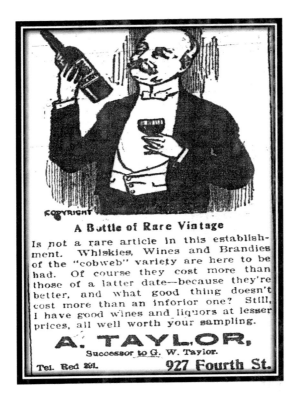

**In 1903 Aged Vintage Wines Were Clearly Marketed to
Upper Class Males and Not the Common Person**

The Volstead Act: America's Failed Experiment With
Prohibition

The dark clouds of prohibition finally turned into a
storm in 1920 with the passage of the Volstead Act.

California wineries as a whole, and San Diego County specifically, suffered over the next thirteen years even as vineyards produced more and more grapes.

During Prohibition grape growing actually increased in many areas of California. The grapes were often sold locally as fruit for small scale, legal home wine making. More importantly grapes were transported by refrigerated freight train as boxed fresh fruit, or pressed into blocks of must or juice and shipped to the East Coast for home winemakers. San Diego County reflected this growth and went from 4,340 acres of vines in 1914 to 7,370 acres in 1920.

The acreage for 1925 was even more impressive with San Diego having 8,264 acres of vines of which 2,410 or 29% were wine grapes. But with the increase in volume, grape prices tumbled from $2.40 a lug (about 35 pounds) in 1921 to $1.07 a lug in 1930.

Destined for wine-deprived home wine-makers, there was little incentive for vineyard owners to produce high quality grapes. Emphasis was placed instead on high yield and the ability of the grapes to withstand long distance shipping. In 1930, the vineyards of California reportedly shipped 50,595 railroad cars of grapes to the East Coast. New York City alone, with its large immigrant population, received 15,766 of those railroad cars. Situated at the end of the rail lines, and without an established reputation for wine grape production, San Diego's vineyard owners and vintners gradually lost much of their economic livelihood.

Certainly some enterprising wineries, including the Rizzo's at Bernardo made so-called sacramental wines. The Ferraras sold tons of grapes for home wine making, and several wineries produced "medicinal" grape juice.

A questionnaire sent out by the federal government to San Diego County grape growers in the summer of 1929 sought to find out where the tons of grapes from El Cajon Valley and elsewhere were going. The responses were predictably surly and witty. One grower wrote, "My mother did not raise me to be a stool pigeon." Another grower of an independent stripe told the inquisitors, "When my attorney advises me that it is unlawful to sell my product in the open market, I shall answer your questions." And finally, one of the largest growers in the County simply and sardonically wrote, "I ate them."[44]

Friends and families of local winemakers always kept a few gallons of wine in their cellars and tucked away in the vegetable bin, but prohibition struck hard at the local wine markets. Illicit speakeasies and private clubs were unlikely to carry California wine; gin, whiskies, beer, and imported Champagne wetted the whistles of the adventurous party goers — not fine wines.

In response to the restrictions of Prohibition most local wine grape growers ripped out their vines, some of which were more than 50 years old and planted fruit and nut trees. Others including Robert Topi tried to sell there vineyards but often there were no takers in the midst of the Great Depression. The rise of the citrus industry in San Diego County also coincided with the decline of the nationwide wine market.

The Prohibition Experiment Runs Dry

Repeal of Prohibition in 1933 led again to a substantial upsurge in vineyards and wineries in San Diego County and all of California. The local market initially proved lucrative while the larger Napa and Sonoma wineries were slow to enter back into the wine business. In 1934, San Diego had ten struggling wineries, but that number soon doubled.[45]

The four older local wineries that survived the dry years, Bernardo, Granchetti, Topi (Einer), and Ferrara, were soon joined by 16 new wineries. These new wineries included Guiseppe Iavelli's in Poway, J. H. Davis' Highland Valley winery and Lewis and Alta Hart's winery in Highland Valley, Joseph Mottino's and

George Borra's Borra Winery on the Isola Ranch in Escondido, Casaran near Lake Wohlford, Flegal Winery (a successor to Brabazon in Alpine), and Vic de Lu (a successor to Bruschi's) in San Diego.

In 1935 San Diego had 2,447 acres of wine grapes compared to 1,600 in 1930--clearly local growers believed that wine and brandy would make a comeback. In an effort to promote local wines and to fight state and federal regulation, the San Diego County Grape Gowers Association came to life in early 1939. Founding members included Borra, Mighetto, and Hart.

Reflecting a florescence of wineries not seen since the 1890s these wineries were spread across the county. Giuseppe Iavelli's winery was east of the intersection of Poway Road and Garden Road near Sycamore Canyon; Vic de Lu made their wine from Alpine grapes vinted at India and Market Streets in San Diego south of Broadway.

The Hart winery began operations in 1935 when Alta and Lewis Hart moved from Burbank, California to the Highland Valley area and opened their winery. The Harts took over an old vineyard that had been planted by William Winn in the early 1890s. Described as a modest operation, Hart's winery sat above and south of San Pasqual Valley, off Bandy Canyon Road. Today the site is occupied by the Espinosa Winery. Nearby to the northeast is the Highland Valley Vineyards.

July 3, 1936 Advertisement for George Borra's Escondido Wines From His Borra Winery

South of the international border, Angelo Cetto immigrated from Italy to Guadalupe Valley in 1927 and soon established L. A. Cetto winery specializing in brandy. Through the efforts of wine maker and vintner Camilio Magoni, an immigrant from northern Italy, L. A. Cetto grew to become one of the major wine producers in Mexico. Magoni used Grenache and Carignan in his wines and nursed full bodied, flavorful wines from the arid valley. Bodega de Santo Tomas Winery opened in 1937 and began purchasing surplus grapes from San Diego County vineyards.

This trans-border vinicultural commerce still flourishes, except in reverse. Some local San Diego wineries, and many amateur winemakers, annually purchase several tons of grapes from the Guadalupe Valley in Baja California.

Post-prohibition prosperity for the San Diego wine industry proved short-lived. World War II spelled yet another decline for local wineries. The downward spiral resulted from rationing, labor shortages, a decrease in wine consumption, and the windfall profits to be gleaned by growing food products for the war effort.

To make matters worse, in the midst of the war, a law was passed in 1943 prohibiting the sale of bulk wines. Many San Diegans, both home consumers and restaurants, still purchased wine in bulk by bringing their own containers to the wineries and wine shops that dotted lower Fourth and Fifth Avenues. The idea of buying wine in increments of less than a gallon was a strange and unpopular concept.

The bulk wine prohibition raised the price of wines, led to the need for increased mechanization at the winery, and placed winemakers in a position of retooling and rethinking how they produced, bottled, and marketed their wines. Adding to the woes of the winemakers, the post-war generation in general did not embrace wine as their fathers and grandfathers had.

In part this was because the post Prohibition, pre-World War II wines were of vastly variable quality. Hard liquor and beer became the alcoholic beverages of choice, and sugary soft drinks gained increasing market share with large firms and conglomerates dominating advertising and the marketplace.

Gradually, everyday wine began to fall into two general categories; low class fortified jug wines or high end, usually imported varieties associated with the upper class and special occasions. By the 1950s and into the 1960s there was little middle ground between the jug

wines from California's Central Valley wine lake and
the aged wines from California and France.

**Post-Prohibition Consumers Were Invited to Bring Their
Own Jugs and to Fill Up on Wines That Varied From
19% to 21% Alcohol**

Unfortunately, San Diego's wineries did not fit well into either category and accordingly suffered. By 1940 wine grape acreage in San Diego fell from 2,447 in 1935 to 2,077 and 1,850 by 1945.

Although recently revived, Escondido held its last Grape Day celebration in 1949, a sign of the decreased importance of the grape industry in North County.

From a high of 30 wineries just before prohibition, and 20 wine making operations in the years just after repeal, by 1964 San Diego County could only boast of two locally made wines, Ferrara and Bernardo. The acreage devoted to wine grapes had fallen to a mere 510 acres or less than 20% of what it had been in 1935. The old stalwarts, Bernardo and Ferrara clung on, but the high price of land, upward spiraling property taxes, and water costs would soon shrink them even further.

A book on the wines of California published in 1967 carried ads for only two wineries in San Diego County, Ferrara and Brookside, and Brookside sourced its grapes from outside of the county in the Cucamonga Valley[46]

The mega marketer Brookside Winery, a large scale operation based in Cucamonga with 36 outlets had four retail locations in San Diego County. Brookside claimed to have been established in 1832 although there is no documentation of such an early start. Nonetheless, visitors could go to the familiar faux mission style Brookside outlets in Pacific Beach, Bonita, El Cajon, and Escondido and taste a wide variety of mid-range California wines; but none from vineyards in San Diego County.

Mission Style Architecture Meets 1960s Styles at the Brookside Winery on Highway 395 in Escondido.

In the late 1960s, and in a revival that continues until this day, Temecula came on to the wine scene. Brookside, and almost simultaneously Vince and Audrey Cilurzo, planted the first commercial vineyards in Temecula in 1968 for their winery now known as Bella Vista.

In 1971 the first wines from Temecula grapes were released by Brookside, who actually vinted the wine at their Cucamonga facility. The wine market in the 1970-1980 period was dominated by sweet wines and the ubiquitous, well-advertised wine coolers — think Bartles & James!).

Note the Architectural Alterations that Transformed the Escondido Brookside Buildings from Faux Mission Style to Faux English Tudor for Canterbury Gardens Gift Shops

By July 1986 even Brookside was out of business although they are making a comeback today as Gen7Wines with a descendant of the original owners at the helm.

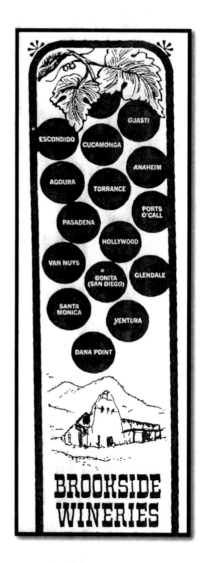

Advertisement for Brookside Wineries Circa 1967 With
the Escondido and Bonita Locations Shown

Summary

From its humble origins during the Spanish colonial period at Mission San Diego circa 1781 wine and wine making in San Diego County has reflected the history of the county. It is a story of immigrants, of failed crops, Indian labor, the effects of the Volstead Act from 1919 to 1933, floods, fires, and urban growth.

The historic heyday for San Diego County wineries was probably the 1890s era and then again immediately following Prohibition in the mid-1930s. The wines of San Diego have always reflected the economic status of the region, the varied ethnic blends, and of course, the land itself.

The table on the following page lists the major wineries and vineyards of San Diego County and northern Baja California between 1781 and 1937. Certainly there were more but these are the ones with a true place in history and that appear in the directories and advertisements of the times

Winery/Vineyard	Locale	Founding
Mission San Diego	San Diego	1781
Agoston Haraszthy	North County	1850
Maxcy	Valley Center	1867
Marco Bruschi	San Diego	1870
Juan Forester	Santa Margarita	1872
Emmanuel Daneri	Otay Valley	1878
Theophile Verlaque	Ramona	1879
Rufus K. Porter	Spring Valley	1884
Phillipo Poggi	Otay Valley	1885
Guatelli	Otay Valley	1885
Philip Brabazon	Alpine	1888
M. C. Woodson	Ramona	1890
William Warnock	Ramona	1890
Bernard Etcheverry	Ramona	1890
Frederick Schepelle	Alpine	1890
Frederick Einer	Escondido	1890
Lanza Winery	Escondido	1893
Frederick Grand	Julian	1895
George Kuchel	Escondido	1900
G. G. Merriam	San Marcos	1900
George Ferrara	Escondido	1919
Vincenzo Rizzo	Escondido	1927
L. A. Cetto	Guadalupe Valley BC	1930
Giuseppe Iavelli	Poway	1933
Hart Winery	Highland Valley	1935
George Borra	Escondido	1935
Santo Tomas	Santo Tomas BC	1937

The San Diego Wine Scene Today: Healthy and Thriving

Today, in the early 21st century, the wine scene in California, and importantly, in San Diego and Riverside Counties, is robust and growing yearly. From lows of only 77 acres in 1992 and 88 acres of wine grapes in 1975, San Diego County has unevenly increased to 225 acres in 1980 and more than 1,200 acres in 2015. Of all of the old time wineries in the county only the historic Bernardo Winery has survived. The winery currently occupies a 5-acre plot and produces a relatively small 4,000 gallons a year, mostly from grapes sourced in Madera County and from throughout San Diego County.

San Pasqual Valley has long been vineyard country with successive owners of first Jaeger, then San Pasqual, and now Orfila Winery. Orfila's quality Syrah, Sangiovese, and Viognier reflect the new varietals. A new manifestation of the San Pasqual Winery now graces the landscape with outlets in La Mesa and at Seaport Village.

Just up the road from Mount Woodson and the long gone vineyards of old Doc Woodson, Ramona (which now has official AVA status as the Santa Maria Valley American Vinicultural Area) has the greatest number of vineyards and wineries in San Diego County with more than fifteen tasting rooms.

These mostly boutique sized wineries include Schwaesdall Winery, Hatfield Creek, Edwards, Mahogany Ranch, Pamo Valley, and others. To the east of Ramona the Milagro Winery is making award-winning wines; Julian proudly hosts Menghini, Witch Creek, and Volcan Mountain (previously J. Jenkins); the Warner Hot Springs region has Shadow Mountain Winery (with 55-year old vines continuing a heritage begun by Italian immigrants August and Helen Mase), and Emerald Creek Winery.

In the future the historic Warner Springs Ranch Resort centered on the ancient village of Kupa will boast new vineyards thus reviving wine grape growing that took place there in the early 1900s. Escondido has returned to the wine scene with Belle Marie and others.

As surely as the older venerable wineries have been reduced and shrunk, a new breed of wine makers and vineyard owners are springing forward. San Diego County is home to more than thirty wineries and nearly sixty vineyards with new ones starting up every year. The Temecula Valley, once part of San Diego County before it broke off to join Riverside County, and a relatively recent entrant in the wine derby has more than 25 wineries and has gained a reputation for producing several medal winning wines.

In addition to Bella Vista (which was Cizurzo Winery for many years and was Temecula's first commercial vineyard established in 1968 and the third bonded winery) other wineries in the Temecula region have a long history. These include Callaway (Temecula's first bonded winery), Mount Palomar (second), Filsinger (fourth), and Hart (fifth). Temecula Valley Vineyards operates the extensive vineyards once owned by Brookside.

Together, these older wineries and other newer ones in Temecula are becoming well known and respected after some rough spots and false starts. In retrospect, Jules Vignes' dream of Temecula and Cucamonga wine country came true--it just took one hundred years longer than he may have hoped.

In San Diego County new wineries are started every year and back country hills and valleys are literally sprouting young vineyards. Within the more populated portions of the county urban wineries are springing up continuing a tradition begun by Bruschi and Einer over a hundred years ago.

With its long history of producing French and Italian wine varietals, San Diego is poised to take its place in the surging Rhone style wine craze and the Cal-Italia surge. Escondido, Ramona, Fallbrook, Campo, Dulzura. and Julian may never be Sonoma or Napa, but they can become something in the wine world that is uniquely San Diego County.

Taking a Trek into the Past: Visit the History of San Diego County Wineries

Want to take a trek around the county and visit some of the historic vineyards and wineries of San Diego? Sadly much of the physical legacy of our wines and wineries has been destroyed but there are buildings and places that may still evoke a little of the past. Most of the historic winery locales are near current wineries that offer wine tastings so learn a little about the past while enjoying San Diego County wines of the present. Go to specific web sites to check hours and special events for the various wineries and stay abreast of new openings.

The Emmanuel Daneri Building at 532 Fifth Avenue in the Gaslamp District of downtown San Diego is well-maintained and along with adjacent buildings conveys some idea of mercantile San Diego in the early 1900s. His Otay winery can be viewed only by peering through a chain link fence in what appears to be an open space area along the Otay River.

The Brookside Wineries in El Cajon, Escondido, and Bonita all still exist although they have been converted to other uses. The El Cajon structure is largely unchanged and is now used as a dental office at the corner of Arnele and North Johnson. The Escondido facility is home to Canterbury Gardens Gifts at 2402 South Escondido Boulevard and has been remodeled to reflect an English Tudor theme. The Bonita location houses a bicycle shop.

The Brookside Winery in Bonita as it Appeared in the 1960s. Now Occupied by Performance Cyclery

The Bernardo Winery located at 13330 Paseo Del
Verano North in the San Diego community of Rancho
Bernardo is still a working winery with a gift shop and
other shops within the old winery footprint. Head a
little further up I-15 and visit the Vesper Winery or the
Belle Marie winery.

Tie in a trip to this region with tastings at the nearby
wineries along the Highland Valley/San Pasqual Valley
region. Or visit the Ramona Historic Pioneer Society
Guy Woodward Museum and take a tour of wine
pioneer Theophile Verlaque's house.

Once in the Ramona Valley, also known as Santa Maria
Valley, a wide-variety of wines await you including the
Schwaesdall Winery, Mahogany Ranch, and Salerno
wineries on the west side. In town and to the east of
town there is Hatfield Creek, Edwards, and Pamo
Valley among others — check out the Ramona Winery
Association web site for hours and locations.

As long as you are in the Ramona region, venture
further east and head out to the Warner Springs and
Julian area. In this region you will be near the old
Fredrick Grand homestead below Julian and the Warner
Springs Ranch Resort that once boasted acres of grapes.
After you visit Milagro off of Highway 78 drive
towards Santa Ysabel and then north through the

beautiful Valle de San Jose and Warner Springs. Stop at the Warner Springs Ranch Golf Grill for a good sample of very local wines. Or travel towards Temecula along the scenic Butterfield Stage route, now Highway 79, and stop at Sierra Roble, Shadow Mountain, Hawk Watch or Emerald Creek. Other wineries in the area are available by advance appointment.

Or instead of heading north on Highway 79 off of Highway 78 at Santa Ysabel (think Dudley's Bakery) continue east and visit historic Julian and its wineries. In town you can walk in the steps of old man Grand who trotted his wines up there in the 1890s. Sample local wines at Witch Creek, Menghini, Orfila, Volcan, and others.

If you travel through the area served by Highway 94 you can visit the "Wineries of Highway 94." The Westfall Winery is in the historic Buckman Springs area. In the Dulzura area drop by Casi Cielo Winery or Granite Lion Cellars. Near Lyons Peak and Lyons Valley you can visit Deerhorn Valley Vineyards and Dulzura Vineyard. You can also go to Campo Creek Vineyards and in doing so visit the winery that is closest to Mexico.

San Diego has a rich and colorful history of wine making and wine drinking. Make a little history of your own and enjoy a glass or bottle of our local wine.

Partial Listing of San Diego County Wineries

Most of these wineries have web sites and the web sites should be consulted for up to date information on hours, availability, and events.

Members of the San Diego Vintners Association (SDVA)

Winery & Representatives

Winery	Representatives
Accidental Winery	Sanders, Donald "Mike"
	Chris Ambuul
Altipiano Vineyard & Winery	Clarke, Peter & Denise
Beach House Winery	Murray, George
	General Information
Belle Marie Winery	Lazenby, Jeff
Bernardo Winery, Inc.	Ross Rizzo Jr.
	Sam Nowracki
	Selena Roberts
BK Cellars Urban Winery & Tasting Lounge	
	Joe Ames
	Dania Ames, General Manager
Brooking Vineyard	Eric Brooking
	Private email address

Campo Creek Vineyards	Bill Clarke
	Mary Clarke
Carruth Cellars	Adam Carruth
Casa Tiene Vista Vineyard	Susan Gallagher
	Mick Gallagher
Cordiano Winery	Gerry & Francesco Cordiano
Coyote Oaks Vineyards	Sherman, Karen J.
Deerhorn Valley Vineyards	Dianne Collis
	Robert Collis
Domaine Artefact Vineyard & Winery	LaChapelle, Lynn
	Robinson, Mark
Dulzura Winery -	Terry Winnett
	Grant Spotts
Eagles Nest Winery	Dennis & Julie Grimes
Emerald Creek Winery	Rao Anne
	Ashley Ammann
Estate d'Iacobelli (dba Iacobelli Wineries)	Ron & Lisa Iacobelli
	Sascha la Russo (tasting rm manager)
Fallbrook Winery	Ted Gourvitz
	Christna Smith
	Izaac Villalobos
Gianni Buonomo Vintners	Keith Rolle
Granite Lion Cellars LLC	Alma T. Hammon

	Sarah Babine
	Grant Spotts
Hacienda de las Rosas Winery	Tammy Rimes
Hellanback Winery	Paula Payne
	John York
Highland Hills Winery	Rich McCLellan
	Theresa McClellan
Highland Valley Vineyards	Schnorr, Ray
	O'Brien, Jeannine
Hill Top Winery	Mike Schimpf
	Cindy Schimpf
	Liz Kasten
Hungry Hawk Vineyards & Winery	
	Embly, Jeannine
	Embly, Ed
	Embly, Mike
Kohill Winery	Mike & Aurora Kopp
Koi Zen Cellars	Lisa Miller
	Darius Miller
La Finquita Winery & Vineyard	Koehler, Charles
Lenora Winery	Eric Metz
Little Oak Winery	Sportsman, Richard
	Rachel Speck
	Taylor Likins
Mahogany Mountain Winery	Kim Hargett

Maness Vineyards & Casi Cielo Farm Wines	Greg Maness
	Paula Maness
	John Keily
	Lissy Keily
Mattucci Winery	Paul & Stephanie Mattucci
Milagro Winery	Barba Winstead
	Alex Guss
Myrtle Creek Vineyards	Matt Sherman
Négociant Winery	Zane Mumford
	John Rinaldi
	Todd D'Alessio
Old Coach Vineyards & Winery	Sandy Mubarak
	Scott Mubarak
	Jason Mubarak
Orfila Winery	Justin Mund
	Donna Gvozden
	Bryan Zamora
Poppaea Vineyard	John Saunders
	Benjamin Saunders
	Marion Saunders
Principe di Tricase Winery	Gallone, Alfredo
	Shelly Hogan
	Raffaella Gallone
Ramona Ranch Winery	Teri Kerns
	Micole Moore
Roadrunner Ridge Winery	Judi Brady
Rock Canyon Vineyards	Timothy Petersen

Salerno Winery	Luisa Rosenfeld
San Diego Cellars	Todd Hipper
	Erica Abraham
San Pasqual Winery	McWilliams, Mike & Linda
Sblendorio Winery	Sblendorio, Phil
	Sblendorio, Laura
Schwaesdall Winery	John Schwaesdall
	Shirley Schwaesdall
Shadow Mountain Vineyards & Winery	Alex McGeary
	Pam McGeary
Sierra Roble Winery & Vineyard LLC	Lowe, David
Sleeping Indian Vineyard	Downing, Troy
	Money, Greg
Solterra Winery & Kitchen	Van Alyea, Christopher
	Chris Powell
	Tiffany Masters
Stehleon Vineyards	Stehley, Al & Lisa
	Fang Zhang (temporary email
Sunshine Mountain Vineyard	& website)
Triple B Ranches	Debbie Broomell
	Chjris Broomell
Turtlerock Ridge Vineyard Winery, Inc.	Laurie Wagner
2Plank Vineyards	Bridgeman, David & Laura
	Mike Szymczak
Twin Oaks Valley Winery	Malcolm & Kathryn Gray
Vinavanti Wines	Eric Van Drunen

Vino Urbano Urban Winery	Harold Dreis
	Teresa Forcier
	Olena Senchuk
Vineyard Grant James	Susanne Sapier
	Nicole Warady
Volcan Mountain Winery	Hart, Jim
	Melanie Shaffer
	Christine Hart
	Mike Hart
Witch Creek	Skip Coomber
	Ryan "Scotty" Scott
Woof 'n Rose Winery	Steve & Marilyn Kahle
Wyatt Oaks Winery	Gavin McClain
	Stacy McClain
ZXQ Vineyards	Andrew Klotz

Selected Wineries Listed By Region

The following list is not by any means inclusive and in fact cover less than one-third of the more than 115 wineries and vineyards in the county. The geographical grouping is from the author, not the owners or geographers. The listed wineries are those that best represent the specific region, the terroir, and/or are generally open to the public.

Ramona/San Pasqual/Highland Valley
Cactus Star
Carossa
Chuparosa
Cordiano
Domaine Artefact Vineyard & Winery
Eagles Nest Winery
Espinosa
Highland Hills Winery
Highland Valley
Kohill
Lenora
Mahogany Mountain
Orfila
Pamo Valley
Pyramid
Salerno
San Pasqual Winery
Schwaesdall
Witch Creek
Woof n Rose

East Ramona/Santa Ysabel/Julian
Edwards
Hatfield Creek
Hellanback
Menghini
Milagro
Vineyard Grant James
Volcan Mountain Winery

East and South County
Campo Winery
Casi Cielo Winery
Deerhorn Winery
Dulzura Winery
Granite Lion Cellars
Westfall Winery

North County/Warner's Valley
Belle Marie
Bernardo
Emerald Creek Winery
Fallbrook
Hawk Watch
Shadow Mountain
Sierra Roble
Vesper

Photo Credits
Research archives of Richard L. Carrico for pages 4, 6, 9, 17,22, 37, 39, 42, 44, 59-61, 67, 71, 74-76, 81, 86, 88,-89, 91, and 93. John Dietler for page 11. Wallace Elliott for page 13. Sacramento State Library for page 16. Valley Center Historical Society for page 24 and 28. Escondido Public Library Pioneer Room, Ryan Photographic Collection page 26, 63-64 and 68. San Diego Public Library, California Room for page 33. Mike Bryant for page 35. The San Diego History Center for page 38. The Bonita Historical Society for page 41. Fred Grand

for pages 45 and 51. The Ramona Pioneer Historical Society for pages 49 and 52. The Vista Historical Society for page 53, Ancestry.com for pages 57 and 62. The Alpine Historical Society for page 73. The City of Escondido web site for page 92.

Acknowledgements

As with making wine, many hands and minds helped to harvest the information and blend the words for this book.

These lovers of wine and of history guided this book along to a final vintage. In the world of local wine and vineyards, Joe Hart of Hart Vineyards in Temecula and Jim Hart of Volcan Mountain Winery in Santa Ysabel helped out on historic facts and early wineries, Richard Crawford from the San Diego Public Library California Room provided obscure sources and photographs, and the well-researched work of California's preeminent wine historian Charles L. Sullivan was invaluable.

Mike Bryant and others provided photos and documents that greatly aided in telling the fascinating story of our wines and wineries.

Many institutions including the Guy B. Woodward Museum in Ramona, the San Diego History Center, the Bonita Historical Society, the Bancroft Library at

Berkeley, the Valley Center Historical Society, the Alpine Historical Society and the Escondido Historical Society and the Pioneer Room at the Escondido Public Library helped with documents and photographs.

Several good friends shared many a bottle of wine over the course of researching this book and helped edit the final drafts including the intrepid duo of Lisa Hillerman and Susan Xanten. My printers at Full Court Press made the book far better than it would have been otherwise and worked with me closely throughout the final stages of the book.

Any errors or misrepresentations are of course, the product of the author and/or of a glass of wine too far.

Sunset Above Warner Hot Springs

REFERENCES CITED

[1] Charles L. Sullivan. "Wine in California: The Early Years. Wayward Tendrils Quarterly, Vol. 20, No. 2, p. 20-28. For a discussion of wine making in the early years of California see Charles L. Sullivan. *Wine in California: The Early Years: Mission Wines 1698-1846.* Santa Rosa: Wayward Tendrils Quarterly Special Publication.

[2] Sullivan, "Wines in California." p. 27.

[3] Alejandra Milla Tapia et al.. "Determining the Spanish Origin of Representative Ancient American Grapevine Varieties." *American Journal of Enology and Viticulture,* vo. 58, No. 2 (2007), pp,. 242-251; *Wine Spectator* February 12, 2007.

[4] Richard Henry Dana. *Two Years Before the Mast and Twenty Four Years After.* New York: Collier and Son, 1937.

[5] *H.M.S. Sulphur on the Northwest and California Coasts, 1837 and 1839: The Accounts of Captain Edward Belcher and Midshipman Francis Guillemard Simpkinson.* Edited by Richard A. Pierce and John H. Winslow. Materials for the Study of Alaska History, No. 12. Kingston, Ontario: The Limestone Press, 1979.

[6] Griffin. Diary of Dr. Griffin.

[7] San Diego Union, September 1, 1876.

[8] John P. Harrington. Field notes for the Luiseño..On file at the National Anthropological Archives, Washington D. C. and on microfilm as Vol. 3, Reel 115.

[9] Ibid; Philip Sparkman. "Culture of the Luiseño Indians." *University of California Publications in American Archaeology and Ethnology,* Vol. 8, 1908. p.192.

[10] U. S. Federal Census, San Diego County, 1900.

[11] San Diego Union. August 28, 1871, p. 3 col. 2.

[12] San Diego Union Weekly. September 28, 1871, p.4, col. 1.

[13] San Diego Union. November 23, 1879, p. 4 col. 1.

[14] San Diego Union. March 25, 1881, p. 4, col. 2.

[15] San Diego Union. September 8, 1881, p. 2, col. 1.

[16] San Diego Union. September 12, 1882, p. 2, col. 2.

[17] Elliott. *Illustrated History of San Diego and San Bernardino Counties.* 1883.

[18] San Diego Union. October 16, 1883, p. 3, col. 1.

[19] File folders at the Valley Center Historical Society Museum.

[20] Diary of Gregorio Omish. On file at the Kumeyaay Community College, El Cajon, California.

[21] Rush, Benjamin. *Ranchos of San Diego County.* p. 55.

[22] Ibid.

[23] San Diego Union. June 25, 1903, p. 5, col. 3. Superior Court Probate Proceedings, San Diego June 1903.

[24] San Diego Union. April 5, 1872, p.3, col. 3.

[25] Lynne Newell Christenson and Ellen L. Sweet. *Ranchos of San Diego County. Arcadia Publishing*: Charleston, South Carolina, 2008, p. 73.

[26] Immigration and Naturalization Records, San Diego Region, September 14, 1885.

[27] San Diego Union. October 8, 1880, p.4, col. 3.

[28] San Diego Union. November 20, 1881, p. 3, col. 1.

[29] San Diego Union. January 10, 1884, p. 3, col. 2.

[30] Richard L. Carrico. *Images of America: Ramona.* Arcadia Publishing: Charleston, 2011.

[31] San Diego Union. December 20, 1902, p.2, col.3.

[32] Omish Diary.

[33] San Diego Union. September, 1, 1897, p.5, col. 2 and September 17, 1897, p.2, col. 4.

[34] San Diego Union. May 6, 1934, p. 3, col. 1.

[35] U. S. Naturalization Certificates, Frederick A. Einer, September 2, 1892.

[36] Charles L. Sullivan. A Companion to California Wine. University of California Press: Berkeley, 1998, p. 119.

[37] San Diego Union. October 8, 1880, p 4, col. 3.

[38] *San Diego Union.* September 6, 1903.

[39] Omish Diary.

[40] San Diego Union, August 22, 1871.

[41] San Diego Union. October 26, 1882, p. 3, col. 1

[42] San Diego Union, March 1884.

[43] San Diego Union. June 19, 1873, p. 3, col. 4.

[44] "Questionnaires of Drys Raise Grape Men's Ire." *San Diego Union* September, 3, 1929, p. 5.

[45] San Diego Union. January 7, 1934, p. 1, col. 5.

[46] Fred S.Cook. *The Wines and Wineries of California.* The California Traveler, 1967.